A Bite-Sized Life Style Book

Secrets You Should Know About Writing Great Songs

or

How to Fish Downstream from Bob Dylan

Roddy Matthews

Cover by
Dean Stockton

Published by Bite-Sized Books Ltd 2020
©Roddy Matthews 2020

Bite-Sized Books Ltd Cleeve Road, Goring RG8 9BJ UK
information@bite-sizedbooks.com
Registered in the UK. Company Registration No: 9395379

ISBN: 9798683590352

The moral right of Roddy Matthews to be identified as the author of this work has been asserted by him in accordance with the Copyright, Designs and Patents Act 1988

Although the publisher, editors and authors have used reasonable care in preparing this book, the information it contains is distributed as is and without warranties of any kind. This book is not intended as legal, financial, social or technical advice and not all recommendations may be suitable for your situation. Professional advisors should be consulted as needed. Neither the publisher nor the author shall be liable for any costs, expenses or damages resulting from use of or reliance on the information contained in this book.

Song writing is like fishing in a stream; you put in your line and hope to catch something. And I don't think anyone downstream from Bob Dylan ever caught anything.

Arlo Guthrie

Contents

Introduction	**3**
Chapter 1	**10**
The Songwriter's Craft	
Chapter 2	**18**
Bad Songs	
Chapter 3	**21**
Subject Matter	
Chapter 4	**29**
Structure	
Chapter 5	**37**
Song Elements	
Chapter 6	**45**
Chord Sequences	
Chapter 7	**53**
Melody	
Chapter 8	**59**
Lyrics	
Chapter 9	**69**
Creative Practicalities	
Chapter 10	**77**
Approaching the Business	
Twelve Take Aways	**84**

Bite-Sized Life Style Books   85
Bite-Sized Books Catalogue   86

A Spotify playlist containing all the songs referred to can be found at:

https://www.bite-sizedbooks.com/product/Secrets-You-Should-Know-About-Writing-Great-Songs/

Introduction

Anyone can write a song. You don't need musical education, or even an instrument. All you need is a voice and an idea. Song writing is fun and it can be very fulfilling. But if you want your songs to make you money, they have to be good.

This book is designed to help you write better songs, by showing you how to improve what you do at all the most important points in the song writing process. It also carries a little advice about presenting your songs to the music industry, which is a vital step if you want to make a living from what you write.

We can begin by taking a brief look at creativity.

All creative activities involve four unavoidable questions. What shall I do, how do I start, what do I do next, and when is it finished? Everything in this book is designed to help you answer these questions.

Next, to understand how to write better songs, we should really ask what songs are *for*. If we understand their function, we will be better placed to design them.

The basic purpose of a popular song is to combine fresh sounding music with words that express shared sentiments or common experiences. Successful songwriters take something familiar and render it newly compelling. The ultimate objective is to forge a connection between a singer and an audience, and that mission starts with the *writing*.

Two important points.

One, song writing is not about feeling your pain – everyone does that. The trick is to write about your pain in a way that illuminates other people's understanding of their pain.

Two, what is popular does not remain constant. It wears out. Popular song is therefore constantly evolving – with changes in rhythms, vocal styles and subject matter. This opens up opportunities for every writer.

It also means that the music business is always a little confused. It wants to produce more of the same, because it's popular, but it also wants to find something different, that will stand out. For writers, the trick is getting to the different stuff at the right time – not too early, when it might sound strange, and not too late, when it no longer carries the charm of novelty.

In popular song, new is always better than old. Having said that, combining familiar elements from the past is a good way to forge a style for yourself. Don't ignore your roots. Value them. Nor is it necessary to invent new music from scratch. The work of successful songwriters shows how plundering older styles can create dynamic hybrids. The future is always buried in the past.

All the scales, chords and rhythms we use today are long established. Your task is to make a distinctive blend out of what we know is effective. This process has been at the heart of popular music since the 1950s. All the biggest selling acts from Elvis to Ed Sheeran have developed hybrid forms of music, drawn from diverse sources, then honed into characteristic styles with impact and appeal. The point is not to create new music, but new mixtures.

This process helped pave the way for hip-hop – the most blatant example of musical recycling – which grew entirely out of repurposing bits of old records as 'loops' to make new combinations.

In the longer term, hip-hop has been immensely influential all across the music industry. It has changed production styles, business models, fashion, and the writing process itself.

Paradoxically, while moving us forward, it has also grounded us in the past: all previous recordings are now relevant.

But above all, the use of loops massively increased the amount of repetition to be found in pop records since the 1980s. Repeating chunks of music exactly gave records a new sonic quality, which weaned the public off older styles of rhythm section, where every bar was slightly different because it was played by humans in interaction.

That kind of shimmering mosaic was abandoned for something harder and sharper when dance music began to use entirely computerised tracks. Drum machines and samples had a heaviness of their own which owed nothing to the quality of the classic funk favoured by early hip-hoppers.

As musical repetition became easier to create, or perhaps just harder to avoid, contrasts were minimised and pop music became increasingly uniform and cyclic. The need, then, was for ways of injecting variation, and the obvious answer was via the voice. But that produced its own problems.

While ninja singers could inject all sorts of excitement over repeated patterns, vocalists with less range slowly lapsed into a mixture of rapping and monotone, pitch-corrected singing that took most of the melodic movement out of the vocal line for the sake of pure rhythm.

This is where we are today. Musical repetition has largely triumphed over variation, though this is likely to be only a temporary victory, because of a very simple truth. Music without variation is boring, while music without repetition lacks meaning.

Accessible music has to contain a blend of both repetition and variation.

Repetition gives structure, allowing the listener to enjoy the return of familiar content. It also makes rhythms work; dancers can't dance freely if they are not sure where the next beat is falling.

But repetition has its drawbacks too. Very repetitious music is dull, and most people's experience of extended repetition is unpleasant; without contrasts, music lacks shape. Therefore, a degree of variation is desirable, especially if we are expected to join in. It is also variation that gives music its narrative quality, allowing a song to have a recognisable beginning, middle and end. If used excessively, variation produces confusion. But kept within bounds, it is the essential flavouring that retains our interest as listeners.

So, how can repetition and variation be kept in appropriate balance? There is no single answer to this question, and when we look at different genres we find different proportions. Jazz tends to prioritise variation, and dance music favours repetition. But this dilemma has been solved by both classical and pop music in exactly the same way.

The great classical composers built up melodies from repeated rhythmic phrases (motifs), which vary in pitch more than meter. The opening passages of Beethoven's Fifth Symphony, or of Mozart's Fortieth (K 550), are perfect illustrations. But be aware: it is the variation of pitch that makes the genius of the composition. It tricks us into ignoring the repetition of the rhythm.

The first great secret of song writing is to use repetition of form with variation in content. This combines regularity, which gives structure, with changing content, which maintains interest.

Keeping a balance between repetition and variation is very much the key to successful popular song writing. Having a good idea is not enough. If you use unadorned repetition, even a good idea will irritate very quickly. Well-judged repetition works as a roadmap for first-time listeners; it tells us where we are within a song, which usually enhances our enjoyment. And judicious use of repeated words will probably let your listeners know what the title of the song is, which is a desirable thing, commercially speaking.

To understand how this works, sing *Happy Birthday* to yourself. As the most successful melody ever written, it surely has something to teach us. All four of its lines start with the same rhythm built on the same words, and lines 1, 2 and 4 are identical rhythmically and lyrically, though they vary in pitch. Line 3 is longer; it does not finish on the first beat of the (three beat) bar, but on the second, after the addition of one extra note. This is the pivotal point of the tune, and the place where a new chord is introduced. The melodic shape of all four lines is distinct, with the first two lines mirroring each other very closely.

Note that the verse melody of *bury a friend* by Billy Eilish conforms closely to these rules of cellular repetition and variation.

Recent pop writing, however, tends to minimise variation, like *Sunflower* by Post Malone and Swae Lee, or *Truth Hurts* by Lizzo, both of which use identical vocal patterns multiple times, over a repeated bass movement.

But there are many possible ways to combine repetition and variation. Most obviously, you can repeat words while changing the melody, as in *Happy Birthday*, or repeat a melody using different words, as in hundreds of pop verses, such as *Hold My Hand* by Jess Glynn. More subtly, you can take just the rhythmic shape of a phrase and repeat it with different words *and* melody, as in the chorus of *Never Gonna Give You Up* by Rick Astley, or *God Save the Queen*.

Or you can take a vocal phrase, identical in melody and lyric, and position it at different points within the bar. The opening vocal line of the chorus of *Irreplaceable*, by Beyoncé – "You must not know 'bout me" – appears twice, first on beat 1½, then on beat 4½. Blink 182 also used this technique in *I Miss You*. In the chorus, a higher voice sings the same two-note motif five times in a row, starting on different beats of the bar each time. A lower voice then sings the song's title twice, with the same melodic shape starting on different beats.

Taylor Swift's *Shake It Off* and Lady Gaga's *Stupid Love* both make good use of this kind of displaced repetition, and in *Umbrella* Rihanna is absolutely shameless with it. For a classic masterclass, seek out *Rock And Roll* by Led Zeppelin.

Repetition of form and variation of content – i.e. recycling identical ideas in fresh ways – can be found absolutely everywhere in all popular music, from Stephen Foster in the 1850s down to today.

As a first indispensable tip, I recommend that you learn to spot it, then consciously include it in your own writing.

Everyone else does.

Chapter 1

The Songwriter's Craft

Where do songs come from? How can you start to write?

To get a grip on this, first we need to look at the myth of inspiration – the idea that writers are not really making choices but are merely obeying some outside force. If you, as a writer, sit around waiting for inspiration, you could be waiting a long time.

Successful writers are more proactive than that. If they don't have an idea, they go looking for one, and keep looking till they find a good one. Inspiration is just a temporary state of certainty about what to do. It enables rapid activity without reflection. But this is not the normal condition of writing. Moments of inspiration account for only a small percentage of a writer's life. The rest is hard work.

Carry a notebook, sing into your phone, listen to conversations on the bus and in the street, watch trashy television, read agony aunt columns, adapt proverbs and current catchphrases, use in-jokes and slang from your close social group, scan magazine headlines, listen to old songs, adapt a classical or folk melody. Ideas are around you all the time. You just have to make a little effort to pick one out.

Another very good tip is to collaborate. That way you can pool your skills, inspire each other and edit each other's ideas.

But how do you begin?

Decision one. Should you start with words or music?

Sometimes this dilemma solves itself. For instance, if you are asked to write a song for a film or TV project you will generally be working backwards from a title. Or, if you are writing within certain styles, like house music, you will be working with a fixed tempo, and music must come first, because if that isn't right, nothing else will be.

But the really key element of a song is its melody, and many highly successful writers start with a tune. The Bee Gees and Abba did; Max Martin does. That way your melody and your music are very closely integrated. Working with a singer who can improvise vocal lines as the music is coming together is a great help. Then you can approve the vibe of the song on the spot, without having to bother too much about its detailed meaning. This keeps up the excitement in the room, and allows musical content to be completed very quickly.

If you write alone, you may well come up with words and music at the same time. Sting does this, and it gives your song shape and meaning early on. Writing can then feel more like a process of management than an open-ended struggle.

Working in teams can also render the issue redundant. Backing tracks are now often completed by one set of writers, then given to 'top liners', who provide all the vocal elements. This is a rather industrial approach which treats vocal content as something of an add-on, and reduces the chances of producing a truly integrated pop song. But it shrinks distances, which gives more people a chance to write, and it is generally faster, which makes better use of studio time.

Good songs can be written the other way around. Bernie Taupin always gave finished lyrics to Elton John, and some rock bands have followed this model, including Squeeze and Manic Street Preachers. However, there are few other consistently successful examples of this method in pop writing.

Modern practice has also blurred the lines between writing and production, which isn't a particularly healthy development. Concentrating on presentation at the expense of the basic material risks undervaluing the writing, and you may end up carefully polishing a turd. Sometimes recording a basic guitar or vocal demo on a phone, and/or writing lyrical ideas on a notepad is a better way to start than trying to build a killer track – if you want the end result to have a coherent pop sensibility to it.

And this is really the key. If you consider yourself a serious writer, you may well value words more than music. In which case, write words first. If you think of yourself as creating pop music, concentrate on setting good melodies against convincing music, and let your words come when they will.

Decision two. Should you originate or emulate? Everyone in popular music copies, to some degree. There is always a style, an artist, a song that you have in mind. But within those limits, there are rules of prudence.

One: direct stealing will get you into trouble over copyright.

Two: close copying means that you will always be one step behind everyone else and the best you can hope for is a second-class living.

Three: if your imitation is too slavish, you bypass the process of understanding what you are doing. If you copy individual lines, you will not understand how to develop them. If you imitate a whole song, you will need another model to write another song. All this will leave you incapable of taking your writing much further, and there may be too little of yourself in the end product to make it interesting to anyone else.

The lesson of history is that a degree of imitation is inevitable but that it is better to get it slightly wrong, by accepting, or even celebrating, your own limitations. Most of the big successes of the modern era have been rooted in imitation. The Beatles copied numerous American artists, and Lady Gaga took some time to live down the 'new Madonna' tag.

Although there are plenty of models to choose from, the next valuable secret is that your best source of originality is your own personality. Use what you know. Be yourself.

A full-blown commitment to originality is not necessary. The fundamentals of pop music's appeal have not substantially changed in decades. Despite fashions in rhythm patterns, tempo, instrumentation and vocal styles, the best pop is still novel, danceable and relevant to the concerns of young people.

The demands of the industry have not changed either. It needs standard output to maintain business as usual, but it also yearns for artistic quality, which means business not as usual. You can choose which need to supply, but don't fret unduly about it; good songs speak for themselves.

To keep all this in perspective it is worth reflecting on what you actually want from your writing. If you want the whole package – mass acceptance, critical acclaim, wealth, and real control over your own destiny – the best way to secure it is by carving out your own niche. Adele was never the new Whitney Houston; she was always Adele.

Decision three. All songs have words, so you must take a view about lyrical content.

Lyrics are important because they give you cross-cultural access to buzzwords, youth fashions and current issues. They also act as an entry to philosophy, be it homespun and folksy, or radical and literary. Beats and melodies give energy; lyrics give depth, and allow the artist to appear wise and not just fashionable.

Lyrics are also centrally involved in a song's memorability, particularly by titles. Old school writers used to say that a song with a good title writes itself. Not entirely true, of course. A good title can help you write a song, but don't try too hard. Ask yourself: how many songs have you liked just because of the title? Generally, a pop lyric should be concise and stick more or less to the same stance throughout; as with music, a lyric is most powerful when it sends one message. Pop songs are better at expressing the intense emotion of a single, focused moment – a snapshot – than addressing a series of different subjects or views.

Occasionally a duet will contain real dialogue, and even less occasionally the two voices will have different outlooks. This worked brilliantly for Gotye in *Somebody That I Used to Know*, but there were actually two lead voices on that record. Would it have been as effective with just one?

In a lyric, statements, either positive or negative, work better than questions. Statements can bear repetition more than questions, largely because a question without an answer, especially when asked repeatedly, has diminishing force.

You can tell stories, but if you do, your story must be clearly told and easy to follow.

Whatever your choices, the aim is still to hijack around three minutes of your listeners' attention, to supply an experience that uplifts or moves them, and leaves an emotional impression.

Song writing defies analysis in many of its aspects – even great writers find it difficult to explain what they do – but there are some basic good practices.

Maintain musical simplicity, but without undue crudeness. A degree of predictability helps create satisfying structures, but raw repetition is fatiguing.

Convey excitement, but don't overload your listeners; guide them, entertain them.

Like actors, singers can inject extra intensity into their tone of voice, but writing is a cooler science than the fiery art of performance. Keeping the two separate is essential. This is a roundabout way of saying that shrieking hysterically in search of a melody is not a good way to write a song. A good song is more than a moment in a singer's voice. The best songs are the ones that anybody can sing.

Though spontaneity is often a friend, the process of writing is principally one of calculation, dealing with the constant, inescapable choice of whether to do the same thing again or to do something different. Both musically and lyrically, repetition is the simplest form of emphasis available to a writer.

But – what kind of repetition?

Be aware that many of the most useful forms of repetition are not exact but disguised, so that similar material is presented in new ways, thus slipping past our conscious mind's resistance to the tedium of pure repeats.

As an exercise, listen to a favourite song and write down how many repeats, and types of repeats, you hear. I guarantee that there will be a great many more than you expect. Count how many times lyrical repeats occur, and notice whether they use the same notes, and if they appear in the same position within the bar. Doing this will tell you as much about structure in song writing as you need to know.

Repetition can stultify the senses – trance music is aptly named – so songwriters must avoid this numbing effect while using repeats for structure and emphasis. Here is the secret of melody; that melodic phrases benefit from repeated rhythms. Essentially, in good melodies and arrangements, we are listening to the same patterns over and over, but we are also being refreshed by the distribution of pitch, rather than rhythm. Your mantra should be to repeat rhythm and vary pitch.

You can also selectively repeat some words but not others. Repeating the beginning of a line can be very effective, both within and across verses; it sets up a model that a listener can easily follow, and gives definite shape for a writer to develop. Or adding an identical tag after different verse lines can help pull the variations back into a recognisable place.

Beyond writing, performance also offers a layer of available variation, where the content is repeated, but the delivery is different. This is the very essence of soul singing; the formal content stays the same while extra human energy supplies the variations.

All these techniques have a single central aim – to diminish the amount of repetition from one hundred per cent, to a point where the difference between repetition and variation is hard to nail down. That's when the whole thing flows, with enough weight for memorability yet enough lightness for enjoyment.

To sum up.

Songs are a blend of repeats and changes, all centred round a voice, and that voice is the most important character in the story that is being told.

Imitating what's in the charts is a second-best strategy; the charts won't tell you what is coming next. You will only get noticed if you bring something new.

Combining different types of repetition gives your listeners less information in a more compelling way. This is how 'less is more' actually works.

Keep it simple, make it current, don't worry if it seems obvious, and don't be afraid to put something of yourself into it. The best songs sound like a slice of now.

Creatively we are judged by our peaks, not our average work. So always aim for peaks.

Chapter 2

Bad Songs

To understand why good songs are good, it is worth asking why bad songs are bad.

Good songs have an internal coherence that engages us. They are stuffed with musical and lyrical correspondences – internal reflections – that make them simple to follow, easy to remember and, above all, enjoyable. They set up expectations and fulfil them. They probably tell us something we already know, but they do it inventively, in a way that excites, delights or satisfies us.

Bad songs do not fulfil these criteria. They bore, annoy or confuse us.

By their nature, however, bad songs are a bit of a hidden species. Most people don't get to hear a lot of really bad songs; gatekeepers in the media are paid to weed them out. Unfortunately, this is not the case for aspiring songwriters, who may well be hearing a lot of bad material, because they are writing it.

It is difficult to tell exactly why your homespun efforts do not sound like the stuff you admire. Ego can blind us in all sorts of ways to our own failings, and excuses are readily available, such as having cheap equipment. But there are certain universal traits that poor material displays.

Bad songs feature predictable ideas and dwell on them for too long. They lack the gift of energy that measured variation brings. They also flirt too closely with cliché. When we hear familiar ideas served up in uninteresting ways, we zone out. Lack of originality is as great a fault as too much.

The other main deficiency of bad songs is in not clearly establishing where our attention is meant to be focused.

Musically, this may be the result of a melody that fails to retain our attention; for example, if the phrases are too long, or lack metric consistency, or the vocal is so embellished that a well-shaped, written line is not obvious.

Lyrically, a bad song may be unclear about how many people are involved in the song's storyline, or at what point in their relationship we have found them, which makes it difficult to understand their dilemmas. Scattering too many pronouns, or changing to whom they refer, are cardinal sins; always make it clear who 'you' is. Incoherence is the enemy: what is this about, who is talking, and why are they happy or upset?

Some ideas are not very interesting. It is up to the writer to recognise this early on and then abandon the work or make changes. There is no disgrace in abandoning work; it is often the best thing to do, and professionals do it all the time. But knowing when to abandon and when to redraft is the skill, and that can only come from developing a set of standards to which you hold yourself.

Another type of bad song is a song that doesn't ring true. This might be because the language used is wrong, such as an attempt to evoke street life that doesn't use convincing street language. If you don't use 'ain't' in your everyday speech, don't put it in a lyric. The same goes for 'baby'.

Excessive demonization of a central character also tends to distort a song's sense of reality. Was he/she really that bad? If listeners suspect that someone has colluded for too long with an abusive person, this may induce sympathy but it is unlikely to generate much enjoyment. Ex-lovers should only be so bad, if we are to stay within the bounds of shared experience. Write about the joy of freedom, not the misery of confinement.

Prolonged repetition is always to be avoided, as it removes any doubt about what is coming next. Bad dance music is usually a two-bar loop extended endlessly, containing well-worn ideas and pre-set sounds. Too much vocal and verbal similarity can be very tedious, in any style.

In sum, a bad song is either boring, dishonest, blatantly unoriginal, clichéd, obscure, too long, overwrought, or poorly focused.

These are technical deficiencies, but in common parlance people can be very loose with their use of the word 'bad'. To most people, a bad song is simply a song they don't like.

The first major reason they may not like it is because they have heard it too often. This is hardly a failing of the writing, and indeed is a bit of a tribute to it. *Brown Eyed Girl* and *Hotel California* wouldn't have been played so many times on the world's radios if they weren't good. But overexposure often turns a song that was once a joy into a cross to be borne. In recent times, *Happy* by Pharrell Williams has turned from an uplifting slice of pop-dance action into a jaw clenching moment of despair.

Massive exposure is both a blessing and a curse, which explains why lists of the ten best songs of the year are sometimes quite similar to lists of the ten worst songs of the year.

There is also a degree of musical snobbery hidden in the good-bad polarity, because successful songwriters are often flirting with the boundaries of cliché. This is generally the area of song writing described as cheesy rather than bad. It is worth being clear about how close to that cheese boundary you are prepared to go.

For instance, Stevie Wonder, undoubtedly one of the greatest popular songwriters of the last century, and a man to whom beautiful ballads came as easily as searing social commentary, wrote at least three massively cheesy songs; *I Just Called To Say I Love You*, *Isn't She Lovely*, and *You Are The Sunshine Of My Life*. All sold well, have enjoyed long lives on the airwaves, and have been covered repeatedly by other artists. Queen had a joyful cheesiness to much of their output, and Lionel Ritchie was always able to move people deeply with simple language. More recently, Coldplay have frequently touched what could be called a common nerve with lyrics that can read like greetings cards.

The options here are like a panoramic landscape. Over to the right there is the controversial, the unsayable, the upsetting, the challenging, while over to the left there is the comforting and the familiar. Those who wish to confront their listeners with the darker side of their natures can all troop off to the right and make mayhem. Meanwhile, those who wish to connect most easily with their audience will move left towards the banality of shared experience. Not surprisingly, the massive sales and the really long-lived songs are all to be found there. How closely writers approach the cheese boundary is a matter of personal taste. How near do you think *Someone Like You* by Adele is to it? Or *Lady In Red* by Chris de Burgh?

Writers navigate this 'commerciality' problem in individual, and sometimes rather inconsistent ways. Do you think *Walk On The Wild Side* is a commercial record or an arty record? Did Lou Reed make a specific choice as he was writing and recording it? Or ask yourself the same question about *Life On Mars* by David Bowie, or *Everybody Hurts* by R.E.M.

Whatever your answers may be, your overall objective as a writer must be to feel easy about what you are doing. It is not a good idea to play tricks with your own sensitivities by trying to write commercial material that you don't believe in. Doing that will draw you straight into bad song territory.

Simplicity is always a virtue in the pop world, as is directness. Commercial material usually has these two qualities at the very least. So if you write about a universal sentiment or situation in a simple and direct style, with good song management – careful use of repeats and awareness of the song's structural narrative – you will be on the way to writing bankable material.

Chapter 3

Subject Matter

Does it matter what songs are about? Yes, it does. Some songs summarise people's feelings so well that they take a permanent place in popular culture and become part of the language. Other songs pass us by like a party, as pieces of fun and frivolity. Not all songs are equal, and their relative standing often depends on the lyrical messages they carry

Music sets a mood but, inescapably, it is words that define what a song is perceived to be about. There are some famous exceptions. *A Whiter Shade Of Pale* by Procul Harum, or *Bohemian Rhapsody* by Queen are often introduced to the debate. Granted, both had very obscure lyrics, but both had powerful atmospheres and sounded different from everything else. A modern equivalent might be *Turn Down For What* by DJ Snake and Lil Jon.

So, what are the best subjects to choose for a song?

According to Pete Waterman, there are only four – I love you, I hate you, go away, come back. This is a good overview, but it leaves out much of what is now allowable. Davey Ray Moor from Bath University School of Music has a shorter but more inclusive list; love, empowerment and dancing. But again, this is hardly exhaustive. The secret knowledge here is that writers have always tried to say the things that people might want to have said for them in a song. Surveys tell us that these include: thank you, I love you, forgive me, I forgive you.

Or you can tell a story, though it can be difficult to cram all the necessary details into the constricted space that a song allows.

To keep matters clear it can help to ask yourself the questions that script writers ask: whose story is it, what do they want, and where is the love? Above all, when telling a story, economy of expression is all. *Wasn't Expecting That* by Jamie Lawson is a good recent example.

Country music has always favoured narrative songs, and the lesson they teach is that your story must carry a real emotional kick. Try *He Stopped Loving Her Today* by George Jones.

Words always matter because they carry *specific* meanings in a way that melodies do not. You can use as much of this power as you wish, but having something important to say has never been compulsory in pop. The hit writers of the 1950s and 1960s were steeped in the idea that songs should be about universal tropes, though this attitude often produced rather anodyne material, memorable now only for a good tune, if there was one.

A brilliant exception would be *Wichita Lineman*, written by Jimmy Webb, which is highly specific in all its references – to place, character, emotion and situation. Yet that song still profoundly affects people who have never maintained a telephone network, because its specifics illuminate generalities that we all understand.

We are introduced to a sad man, miles from anywhere, stuck up a pole, listening to the wind whistling in the wires. We hear an honest account of his emotional life, which is not actually explained in anything like the same detail as his working life. The song unfolds with the revelation that he is not quite fully engaged with his lover, or would-be lover, who may or may not actually be in a relationship with him.

We also never ask why this song was written, and this is the best trick of all to pull off. When a song seems obvious in its content, yet intriguing too, and when we never question its status as a commercial artefact, all the purposes of the songwriter are fulfilled. *Wichita Lineman* is as good an example of mature song writing as you will find. It's not personal, yet it is.

Since the late 1960s, writers, especially performer-writers, have striven to make their writing more personal, by trawling their own lives and loves. Joni Mitchell is probably the best example, but you may not wish to be quite so revealing, and there are other approaches.

Rod Temperton established himself as the poet laureate of nightclubs, finding new extended metaphors that revolved around dance culture. He had great hooks, but no one was more aware of the process of making records for dancing than Temperton. His entire oeuvre, especially his work with Michael Jackson, is a self-referential paean of praise to after-dark fun and the joy of funky music.

Bernie Taupin invented an internal fantasy life for Elton John which propelled him to stardom as a fabricated American with a hankering for the old Wild West. Then, as their careers moved on, Taupin learned to express Elton's real emotional life, albeit indirectly. *I'm Still Standing* was about Elton in a way that *My Father's Gun* or *Saturday Night's Alright For Fighting* were not.

The moral is that you can, and should, write about your own life. It is natural and beneficial to draw on your lived experiences, though it is wise put up a little distance or disguise while doing so.

Some suggestions.

Save your therapy needs for therapists. Song writing is not therapy, it is art. By all means use your life as material; get something good out of a bad experience. But unmediated emotional trauma is not necessarily good art. A song has to be hewn out of the rough material of your experiences. Remember that it is possible to write *about* your experiences without *relating* those experiences. The detail doesn't matter. A lyric line isn't art just because it's true. Extract the core of the feelings surrounding the experience; this is what connects with listeners.

It is not a good idea to experience bad things in order to glean material, so it is wise to maintain a distance between your artistic self and the characters in your songs. The list of writers who failed to do this is full of young people 'taken too soon'. These include Amy Winehouse and Kurt Cobain, whose hypersensitivity left them unable to disentangle their personal and performing lives. Guns N' Roses gained a certain spurious credibility by their ceaseless substance abuse, along with a raft of others, like Mötley Crüe. But none of it ended well, either artistically or health-wise.

Choose subjects to which you can bring some passion; stimulation is a very important part of creativity. Writing should feel like solving a puzzle, or grasping at a new thought. These are high aims, but the best of popular song writing does these things. You are more likely to get to higher heights when taken up in moments of enthusiasm.

Political enthusiasm should, however, be distrusted. Songs are not good political vehicles. They risk descending into sloganeering, and can provoke accusations of naivety, condescension or cynical self-promotion. Party politics should definitely be avoided. More generalised social injustices can make compelling and inclusive subject matter, such as *Dead Boys* by Sam Fender, but if you bring up a complex issue, don't pretend you have a simple answer. Remember, protest songs are a genre; solution songs aren't. And if you want to speak your mind, be sure that you really mean what you say.

Although authenticity is important, it can never be enough to make a song either objectively good or commercially successful. Song writing is not a process of relating real life in an unvarnished manner. Tell stories that describe familiar situations in unfamiliar and illuminating ways. Tell your story in a way that I can make it mine too, either by recognition or empathy.

Madness, the band, were inspired by Jamaican ska, but they resisted purism and infused the music with their own sensibilities. It was just as natural for Suggs to sing about everyday life at school or social discrimination as it was for Desmond Dekker & The Aces to sing about everyday life in the shanty town. Two of the nutty boys' best songs, *Baggy Trousers* and *Embarrassment* were the result. Neither bears a close relation to *007* (*Shanty Town*) or *Israelites*.

Then there is always sex. As a subject it tends to work best when shrouded in metaphor, but the wonders, worries, joys and pains of sexual attraction are an endlessly fertile source of material. Sexual identity can also yield uplifting emotions and, along with gender politics more widely, has become a staple of some genres.

Lastly, drugs have often seemed worthy of celebration in song. *Cocaine*, *Legalise It*, *Golden Brown* and *Can't Feel My Face*, along with a lot of house anthems extolling the joys of ecstasy, have more or less directly addressed the issue of drug use. Few have been as realistic or as scathing as *The Pusher* by Steppenwolf. Approach the whole area with caution.

With subject matter, the ideal is achieving a seamless fit between your small experience and the big musical world you wish to create. Jarvis Cocker did this brilliantly in the later Pulp catalogue.

How can you do it? Two good places to start are what your voice sounds like, and what you want to look like, in terms of the usual components of youth culture – hair, makeup, clothes and dance style. Traditionally, another reliable starting point was always 'influences', in other words what was in your record collection, or perhaps in your parents' collection or those of older siblings. This can get you going, but it risks making you a curator of someone else's history. Rebellion is a better driving force than reverence for what has gone before. You are the raw material: build something out of what you know and what you like.

All the heroes of modern popular music took something from the past – they had to, and many did so with a genuine sense of respect – but the trick is to live definitively in the present. That is what makes new voices relevant, and allows them to ring true. Above all, try to infuse your local context with a sense of self, even if that sense is somewhat exaggerated.

Chapter 4

Structure

Structure is central to the way a song is perceived, particularly on first listening. Poor structure baffles. Good structure regulates pace and directs listeners to what is important. The secret here is that structural issues go far deeper than just the order of major events, like verses and choruses.

There are patterns running through words and music at every level, and laying them out skilfully allows your ideas to hit home with maximum impact. The notes of a phrase, the phrases within a verse, and the various sections of a song all interrelate, especially through forms of repetition and contrast, and it is how these interrelations work together that determines our comprehension and enjoyment of a song. Songs have both big and small bones in their skeletons, and they all count.

In other words, it is the whole structure of the song that affects how 'hooky' it is, not just what comes in the chorus.

How is good structure built?

At its most basic, a writer creates structure by making decisions about whether to do the same thing again or to do something different. In an important sense, structure is therefore just a matter of extended rhythm. Analytically, verse chorus, verse chorus is no different from bass drum snare drum, bass drum snare drum.

But no single structure works universally. The object is to maintain our interest, and it's your taste that decides when and what to change.

Certainly, for the last few decades, the 'verse chorus, verse chorus, middle section, chorus to fade' song structure has been dominant, and it is nicely balanced. But there is nothing sacred about it, and it only developed in the late 1960s. Before that, there were other long-lived formats in popular music. That these are now neglected is not a judgement on their usefulness, it is simply more proof that fashions change.

But all song structures have to cope with certain constraints. The most important of these is that there are deep numerical patterns within music and words that have to be reconciled. These are rarely referred to, but they are absolutely essential to the understanding of structure in song writing.

The main issue is how to marry up music, which naturally falls into divisions of four, with words, which don't. Four-bar musical patterns comfortably multiply into eights, twelves, sixteens and so forth. But words are not so easily marshalled. To keep songs interesting, the neatness of fours in music often needs a little injection of asymmetry from less regimented structures in words.

How to do this well involves understanding a hidden psychology of emphasis and expectation that determines how repeats are perceived.

Identical musical events that happen four times in a row develop a kind of flatness. Psychologically they disappear, or are de-emphasised. This is all right for drums and other background elements, but it is not a good thing in a featured vocal. The time-honoured solution with repeated vocal melodies is to make changes on the third line, to break the flow. Often this third line is extended or somehow twisted so that it takes up the space that a separate fourth line might have taken. As in the choruses of *She Loves You* by the Beatles, or *I Can't Stand Losing You* by the Police.

This 'rule of three' is a fundamental way of managing the expectations of an audience, which is why it also governs jokes that rely on repeated lines for their impact.

Note that if you make a change at the second line, you have side-stepped the problem which the rule of three sets out to avoid. You can then repeat those two lines quite happily, and move on to something else. But if you flout this rule and run three identical lines in a row, there is a very good reason not to go round it a fourth time. If you do, you will relegate its importance. And worse, if you then repeat the whole section, your four in a row becomes a mind-numbing eight.

Anything in a continuous loop will tend to be submerged; our brains are always attracted to the narrative flow of other elements. Three in a row with a twist on the fourth might be called the 'funky rule of four'.

Here we have a clear distinction between foreground and background. The secret is to use the rule of three to govern top-line writing, and the rule of four in instrumental part writing. Why three for features? The rule of three works because you can only make a noticeable difference *after* a repeat. Three lines is the shortest time in which a change can register as a difference. Until there is a repeat, there is no *predictive* structure.

September by Earth, Wind & Fire mixes up threes and fours to good effect. Its featured lines follow the rule of four in the intro and verse, but revert to the rule of three in the chorus.

Uptown Funk provides a virtuoso display of how to manipulate repeats in writing, arrangement and performance. There is constant variation in the delivery of repeated lyric lines, and the only featured four-time repeats come at the end, with the chorus chant. At that point, a cycle of four can work well, because there is no time for it to outstay its welcome.

These rules also work in song formats, which are all ways of trying to create a pleasing sense of variety, while using repeated structures.

Perhaps the best example is the old Broadway musical format known as AABA, used in songs like *Somewhere Over The Rainbow*. AABA has four lines of eight bars each. The first, second and fourth lines use the same melody, with the third acting as a change. This delivers a short but satisfying musical journey. It is also economical, in that there are only two main musical ideas, but they are arranged for maximum impact.

Schematically, AABA is also close to the limerick form of comic poetry. A limerick uses the same structure, with the B section subdivided into two short lines, which rhyme. The A sections – lines 1, 3 and 4 – all rhyme too, but on a different sound. For a musical equivalent, think of *Hickory Dickory Dock*.

Another well-tested structure that successfully integrates threes and fours is the twelve-bar, the format of classic blues. Twelve is three times four, which gives us three musical lines of four bars each. Lyrically, however, a standard twelve-bar contains only two lines. The first is repeated, which gets us up to eight bars, then the last four bars use the second lyric line – the payoff, bringing us up to twelve. One great virtue of the twelve-bar is that, unlike AABA, it dispenses with a balancing last line. Once you've had the payoff, nothing more is necessary.

The modern three-chorus structure has its own, submerged AABA structure, if you count the verse-chorus pairing as an A section, and the middle section as a B. That is why it satisfies us.

There is no pressing reason to abandon the modern three-chorus format. It represents a happy medium between variety, with its range of different sections, and a well-spaced scheme of repeats.

But there are alternatives.

In the 1960s, for instance, two common structures were based around the traditions of folk music. These were, primarily, the AB, or verse-chorus structure, and the verse with tag.

The AB structure is very old, and is so effective it is long overdue a revival.

It can be found in field songs and sea shanties, where a solo singer leads with a line, and everyone joins in for a communal response. Effective use of this was made in Manfred Mann's 1964 recording of *Do Wah Diddy Diddy*, though the song itself was not traditional. It was written by the highly successful Brill Building team of Jeff Barry and Ellie Greenwich, who knew how to steal a good device from the archive.

Lots of folk adaptations in the 1950s and 1960s used AB structures, such as *Tom Dooley*, *Sloop John B* or *The Wild Rover*. We can even find it in very familiar twelve-bar songs, like *Hound Dog*, and *Shake, Rattle and Roll*. At its simplest, it is merely 'this then that', which has a natural rhythm to it. But it can become very predictable. Pop producers and arrangers set to work to minimise this danger, and the AB format plus intros, solos, and key changes was the result. You can find it in *Mambo No. 5* by Lou Bega.

The other major format to emerge from folk music was the verse with tag, which is like an asymmetrical AB structure, but hookier. The tag always uses the same lyric, so the song becomes very memorable, and soon the tag acts as an invitation to join in. This anchoring, in both meaning and melody, allows verse sections to become much more discursive, safe in the knowledge that we are all going to land on familiar ground in due course.

This structure was especially favoured by Bob Dylan, who exploited the lyrical scope it allowed to the very fullest extent, from *Blowin' In The Wind* in 1962, via dozens of examples, including *Make You Feel My Love*, covered by Adele, right down to his 2020 album *Rough And Rowdy Ways*, which contains four examples. He sometimes added extra sections, and generally took the repeated last line not as an invitation to join in but as a chance to ram home a message. It was his ability to be so imaginative and pack such a punch that made Dylan the song writing revolutionary that he was, in terms of subject matter, self-expression and literary quality.

But it wasn't just folk-tinged artists who found the verse-tag structure useful. Several early Beatles songs use a tag structure, such as *I Want To Hold Your Hand*. Smokey Robinson, one of the most prolific and successful American writers of the 1960s, also used it in songs like *Shop Around*, though enhanced in that case with a written middle section and a saxophone solo.

The undoubted merits of the format eventually tempted writers to make the tags longer and more explanatory, so that the A and B sections became increasingly independent. Then, if the A and B sections were in the same key, it began to feel necessary to put something between them, usually to alter the key centre temporarily, so that the return to the original key in the B section felt more satisfying.

Here was the birth of the pre-chorus. Its antecedents can be found in early 1960s songs such as *Please Please Me* or *(I Can't Get No) Satisfaction*, but it had reached full bloom by the time Goffin and King wrote *Natural Woman* for Aretha Franklin in 1967.

Once songs were reduced to movable chunks, the road was clear for multiple new formats. It became acceptable for songs to have three or four different sections which didn't have close harmonic relationships, or natural flow between them. For instance, *You Really Got Me* by The Kinks had three discrete sections in different keys, and *Summer In The City* by the Lovin' Spoonful had four.

Compared to AABA tunes, these songs were patchworks that roamed harmonically wherever they felt like. Here was the seed of songs like *Roxanne* by The Police, or *What A Fool Believes* by the Doobie Brothers, which used regular key changes as part of their dynamic.

Much of this subtlety is currently considered redundant, but the music of the pre-computer era is well worth studying, simply to enjoy the freedom with which writers used to change keys and shift moods to retain the listener's interest. Using variation within songs is not the commercial kiss of death; it may well be the way forward through the 2020s.

The main lesson in all of this is that clear structure is essential in all components of a song, both at the audible 'micro' level of words and notes, and at the more conceptual 'macro' level of sections and formats. A good grasp of this will enable you to extend your writing from simply thinking of short, hooky chunks, to working them up into longer, coherent song forms that feel complete.

Chapter 5

Song Elements

Most of the names for song sections are familiar and self-explanatory – intro, verse, pre-chorus, chorus, middle. All are load-bearing parts of the whole, and none should be neglected. Gradients between them should also be considered – are we going up or down? This can be emphasised later with production and arrangement, but it's best to get shape written into material rather than imposed on it.

I have avoided using the word 'bridge' because it is ambiguous. It can mean a section that comes between a verse and a chorus, or a section in the middle of a song. I have therefore used the terms pre-chorus and middle for clarity.

What follows is an examination of the form and function of five principal song elements, along with hints on how to construct them. Songs do not need all five, but they probably need at least three.

Intro

You have more freedom in constructing your introduction than in any other song section, and your choices matter. It is the first thing that a listener hears, and it sets a tone. So what are the best options?

An intro can use the same music as the verse, perhaps without a full arrangement, like *Dancing On My Own* by Robyn. This is a safe option, smoothing the arrival of the first verse.

Or it can be an instrumental chorus. This is a clever idea, because it allows the chorus to feel familiar when it comes again. Motown writers often chose to do this, as did Rod Temperton, Chic and Stock Aitken Waterman.

Or it can be a full vocal version of the chorus, as in *Sweet But Psycho* by Ava Max.

Or it can be an independent, featured theme. This was a very popular option in the 1980s, as in *Take On Me* by A-ha. More recently the idea has been used by The Chainsmokers (ft. Daya) in *Don't Let Me Down* and The Weeknd, in *Blinding Lights*.

In general, as a result of click culture, modern intros are much shorter than they used to be. So, don't be too long, and strive to catch the ear.

Verse

A verse is a section that appears more than once, with the same music/melody but different lyrics. Choruses declare and assert; verses expand and explain.

Verses are often treated as the poor relations of choruses, but don't underestimate their importance. They make up the bulk of the first minute and a half of your song, so it is wise to get the best out of that time. Hit records usually have good verses *as well as* a good chorus. So don't ramble, hoping that the chorus will save the show.

Don't make verses too long – four lines will do – and never make a second verse longer than the first.

Lyrically, a verse will carry the bulk of the scenario and characterisation in your song. People, places and tenses matter. You also have a choice of rhyme schemes. AABB can sound constricted and predictable; ABCB is much freer.

You also need to think about the phrase length and internal repeat patterns of your verse melody.

You can treat each line as one long unit, or subdivide it into two (or more) shorter ones, which gives more of a sense of pace. Alternatively, long lines can be divided antiphonally into two, with a hook on the end of each, like *Tears In Heaven* by Eric Clapton. This is an old folk form, but still very effective. A version of it appears in *Since U Been Gone* by Kelly Clarkson.

Or you can have three short similar lines followed by an altered or extended fourth, like *Break Up With Your Girlfriend* by Ariana Grande. Or the same, with an instrumental reply, like *Happy* by Pharrell Williams.

If you write your lyric first, you should bear in mind that coming up with a melody for four lines of equal length can be a burden. By the fourth line you may have a real struggle to add interest. So, if you insist on writing four lines of even length, a good trick is to make all the lines melodically different. This is not easy, but Brian Wilson managed it with *God Only Knows*. Examples in other idioms include *La Donna E Mobile*, *Autumn Leaves*, and *Morning Has Broken*.

It is very common to have the first and third lines fractionally longer than the second and fourth. This adds a little unpredictability. An uneven arrangement of 4 3 4 3 feet is called ballad form and goes back a long way: "There is a house in New Orleans/They call the rising sun". It is also the shape of *Land of Hope and Glory*. Descendants of this approach include *Imagine* by John Lennon.

The nearest thing to a golden rule is to place two identical melody lines at the start of a verse. This seems to work very well over looped chord structures. After these twin lines, the listener is set up for a change, of either vocal phrasing or chord sequence, or both. This seemingly rigid discipline actually opens up a great deal of freedom for the writer, and all the greats have used it, including Burt Bacharach, George Michael, Kurt Cobain, Sting and Max Martin. If it's good enough for all of them…

Numerous examples of this structure can be found in the work of Rod Temperton, who used it invariably across the period of his greatest success, from *Boogie Nights*, through *Off The Wall*, *Stomp!* and *Give Me The Night*, to *Thriller*.

No list could contain all the possible verse forms, let alone rank them. The secret is to be self-critical. If you cannot detect strong, clear structure in a verse you have written, rewrite it. Chop the lyrics around till they sing to you. Impose the shape of one melodic phrase on the one that follows. Re-divide four lines into eight, or six plus two. Make even lines alternatively uneven. It is absolutely worth the effort.

The reward of clear structure is that when verse two appears, the listener already knows how it flows, and it acts like a subsidiary chorus – recognizable and reassuring.

The greatest service that repetition does for a writer is to create instant familiarity. Use this in verses as well as choruses. The great writers all do.

Pre-Chorus

A pre-chorus – also called a build, lift, channel or bridge – is a short, optional section which you can insert to enhance the impact of your chorus. There are no rules on when or how you should use a pre-chorus, but here are some guidelines.

A pre-chorus should never be longer than either your verse or your chorus. It will work best if shorter than both. That way it adds variety and injects pace.

It is a good idea to use a different line length and/or rhyme scheme from your verse and chorus, and possibly a different number of lines.

Pre-choruses are most necessary when your verse and chorus are in the same key. If you use different chords in your pre-chorus you get the benefit of a quick diversion from your tonic key in order to make the arrival of the chorus feel like a homecoming. Examples: *I Wish* by Stevie Wonder, *Stupid Girl* by Garbage, *Billie Jean* by Michael Jackson.

Sometimes a pre-chorus can be in the same key as the verse and it simply feature a different vocal approach – a change of meter or register, and/or line length, though in practice this is hard to distinguish from a verse b section. Examples: *Never Gonna Give You Up* by Rick Astley, *Owner of a Lonely Heart* by Yes, or *New Rules* by Dua Lipa.

Above all, a pre-chorus is a bonus, not an obligation. It must serve the song. There is no need to extend your song endlessly. Keep one eye on the clock. Maintain the pace. Get to the good bits.

Chorus

A good chorus should be memorable, uplifting and summative. It helps if it carries the song's title, and the best ones invite listeners to sing along.

Verses are explanatory; choruses are dense and declamatory. No Woman No Cry! YMCA! Celebrate good times! Let's dance! The chorus commands, the verses tell you why you should cheer up/go there/celebrate/dance.

Verses are areas of high variation, choruses of low variation. Compared to a verse, a chorus should have fewer chords, simpler words, more repetition of key words, and a different rhyme scheme and line length. Directness is a prime virtue. Born in the USA! Don't you want me, baby? Watermelon sugar, high!

Using higher notes in the main vocal line is also a tried and tested way to help a chorus stand out. Examples: *Angels* by Robbie Williams, *Leave Right Now* by Will Young, *Dancing In The Moonlight* by Toploader, *Leave A Light On* by Tom Walker.

A good strategy is to create a tightly structured, folk-patterned verse form, followed by a rock-style anthemic chorus.

But above all, try to keep it simple.

Middle

Great writers, from Bacharach-David and Lennon-McCartney right down to Pharrell Williams and Bruno Mars, all put middle sections in their songs. You should too.

A well-constructed middle, of any number of bars, breaks up the predictability of the song's established flow, and prepares the listener for a satisfying return to a familiar section of the song – which can be the verse, pre-chorus or chorus. Sonically, musically and lyrically it offers an opportunity to give relief to the ears and put a twist in the tale. Above all, a distinct middle section sets up a mini re-start from scratch.

Your main choice as a writer, or sometimes as a producer, is whether the middle is written or 'found'.

Story songs, or songs with deep emotions, benefit most from a written middle. If you decide to take this option, you can emphasise the change by adopting a different lyrical angle, or you can introduce a new instrumental theme. It is also a good idea to start on a previously unused chord or to move into a new key, which will gives you the most options for fresh melodic ideas.

Found sections work best in dance tracks. They are created in the studio, using instrumental breakdowns, heavy percussion, chant vocals, and dub echoes. They are basically skeletal rearrangements of the song, designed to maintain its energy with an alternate treatment of familiar elements. This approach dates back at least as far as *Na Na Hey Hey Kiss Him Goodbye* by Steam in 1969, but it came to full fruition in the 1980s. Nile Rodgers was a pioneer and master, as in *The Reflex* by Duran Duran.

Older song formats often used an instrumental solo as a middle section rather than featuring new lyrical or musical ideas. This was a good way of maintaining momentum, but it has largely fallen out of fashion. Over the last few decades, the choice has more often been to introduce a rapper mid-way into a song. This can work in more urban styles, but it is a bit of a cliché by now, and it's not a good idea in less rhythmic genres.

Hooks

Some people call a chorus a hook, but more properly a hook is just something prominent that happens in a song and sticks with you, like the repeated guitar figure in *Music Sounds Better With You* by Stardust, which supplies the majority of the song's charm. A hook is not as easily defined as a chorus; it can be shorter and more irregularly placed in a song, but it usually gives a distinctive character or timbre to a song. Gangnam style anyone?

Ideally, the title of your song should count as a hook. If it doesn't, people may well remember something else about the song, which is not helpful for anyone trying to find it with a view to buying, downloading, streaming or requesting it.

Some songs seem to consist entirely of hooks, which is a salutary reminder that you shouldn't imagine that just one good moment in your song is enough get you a hit. The list might include: *Good Vibrations* by The Beach Boys, *That's The Way (I Like It)* by KC and The Sunshine Band, *Pop Muzik* by M, *Sweet Dreams* by Eurythmics, *Money For Nothing* by Dire Straits, *Get Down On It* by Kool and the Gang, *Ghost Town* by The Specials, *The Message* by Melle Mel, *Slave to the Rhythm* by Grace Jones, *Can't Get You Out Of My Head* by Kylie Minogue, *Single Ladies* by Beyoncé and *Uptown Funk* by Mark Ronson feat. Bruno Mars.

All had attention lavished on them *all the way through*.

Chapter 6

Chord Sequences

The biggest secret about chords is that there is nothing scary or difficult about them. In a song they have two main functions; to suggest a mood or emotion, and to distinguish one section from another. They add tension and release, and lift and drop to your writing.

You can take comfort that all the most effective combinations and sequences are well known, and many of them have been used repeatedly. The real freedom you have is in choosing how quickly you move *between* chords. This aspect of writing – harmonic rhythm or chord frequency – is much easier to understand than any aspect of the theory of harmony, and it is far more important to a songwriter.

This leads us to the truth that if you choose to change chords at the same pace throughout your song, which is currently a very common practice, you are throwing away a very important writing tool.

Bruno Mars uses harmonic rhythm both subtly and effectively. *That's What I Like* uses two-bar changes in the verse, then switches to one-bar in the pre-chorus. *24K Magic* uses different patterns in the verse and pre-chorus. *Rock 'n' Roll High School* by The Ramones relies on only four chords, but within each verse they change with increasing speed, from four bars, to two, to one then to half a bar. If you are only going to use a few chords, move them around intelligently. Even punks could.

Varying harmonic rhythm makes your songs less mechanical and obvious at no cost in terms of groove, while it enhances their melodic possibilities.

There are some things, however, that need to be said about chords, because they take up a disproportionate amount of space in inexperienced writers' minds.

First, the average listener is scarcely aware of them. People hear mood, melody, lyric, rhythm and voices in a direct and instinctive way, whereas chords are like scenery or lighting in a film – an important part of the whole, but not easily distinguishable as a separate element. So, no matter how clever your chords, they are not going to add significantly to the appeal of your song.

The only exception to this is if you use key changes in the right places. These are perceived very directly, and are a proven method of adding uplift. The effects they create are valuable, and cannot be achieved in any other way. It seems wilfully foolish to ignore them and deny yourself the possibilities they offer. For example, *Rock Your Body* by Justin Timberlake benefitted hugely from a key shift in its middle section.

But it isn't worth striving too hard to be original when it comes to harmonic content. It is possible to use entirely conventional chords throughout a career and be successful. Bob Dylan did; it was his attitude and his words that created the fuss. Diane Warren does; it is her combination of memorable words and finely worked melodic shapes that distinguish her work.

No sequence is better than any other. The changes that work best are long established, and they are not copyright material. Many songs are written over the same sequences, like *Wild World* by Cat Stevens, and *It's A Sin* by The Pet Shop Boys. A host of 1950s songs used the 1 6 minor 4 5 pattern, and umpteen used the twelve-bar.

Chords are a very important element of arrangement; players need to know what they are so that their parts fit with each other. But at the writing stage, it doesn't particularly matter which, or how many chords you choose. Using different chords in different sections is a very good way to build strong structure into your songs.

There is something of a myth that modern songs must not include more than four chords. This is complete hogwash. You can have as many chords as you like in a song. There are no limits, though there are rules of prudence.

Some modern records, especially those influenced by hip-hop, have no chord changes at all, like *Bodak Yellow* by Cardi B. But if you do this in a more melodic genre, you will need to create shape by adding vocal and instrumental embellishments, with variations of both pitch and rhythmic patterns. *A Girl Like You* by Edwyn Collins uses only one chord, but musically and sonically the song is highly sophisticated. The same goes for several other well-known one-chord songs including *Once In A Lifetime* by Talking Heads and *Wanna Be Startin' Somethin'* by Michael Jackson.

Writers now commonly run the same chord sequence across a whole song. If you do this you will have to decide how many chords to use. The standard choice is three or four chords in a four-bar turnaround. Using four chords gives balance and regularity, while three opens up more musical space because one of the three has to occupy two of the four bars, usually the last two, and this makes the changes feel less relentless.

But any unvarying pattern places tremendous demands on melody lines and singers. The result has been a fashion to divide cycled songs into at least three distinct sections, each using different vocal registers or tones and different melodic metering. *Good Kisser* by Usher, *Earned It* by The Weeknd, *Dangerous Woman* by Ariana Grande and *ME!* by Taylor Swift all do this, using one, two, three and four chords respectively.

And this isn't just a pop/soul thing. You can find the exact same approach in Nirvana's *Smells Like Teen Spirit*.

The lesson is; if the chords aren't doing the work, the voice has to.

Some chords have come in and out of fashion. Up to the 1950s, the half diminished, or minor 7th flat 5, was ubiquitous, especially as a joining device between sections. Another museum piece is the major seventh chord, which migrated from jazz to pop songs somewhere in the late 1960s, and then sneaked out again about ten years later. Finally, the full diminished chord, though heavily used in both *My Sweet Lord* by George Harrison and *Ghost Town* by The Specials, has not found a place in the charts since *Can't Get You Out Of My Head* by Kylie Minogue in 2001.

Anyone wanting to bring a 'new' flava to their writing should consider adding any of these forgotten chords to their armoury.

But obsession with chords is a very guitar-era thing. Fundamentally, in the modern world, the issue is not chords but bass movement. It's all about that bass. You can dictate the general lilt of your song by shaping how the bass part moves. This gets you away from the imprisoning concept of chords, and allows you to write melodic structure into the lower end of your song as well as the upper.

Lastly, writing a chord sequence is not the same thing as writing a melody. Chords do not imply melodies; melodies imply chords.

If you write a chord sequence and then sing chord tones over each chord as it comes, your melody will have a stop-start effect and will not seem to flow with the whole sequence. If you write a blues/soul (pentatonic) melody over major and minor (diatonic) chords, you are in effect ignoring them, and haven't used them as part of your composition process. Treat melodies as free-standing patterns and they will come out better.

Chord sequences, unlike so many other elements in music, don't have names. Individual chords have names, but the familiar combinations we use do not. This makes it slightly difficult to discuss chord sequences without spelling them out, with major and minor suffixes, which is very dry off the page, and requires a certain amount of experience to hear in your head. This especially applies to the four two-chord cadences which do have names, and can be found listed on Wikipedia.

Pop music generally only uses one of these four: the half cadence, meaning a movement from any chord to the 5 (dominant). The fifth step of the scale is termed the dominant, and a seventh chord built on that fifth step is called a dominant seventh.

The dominant seventh chord has been ubiquitous as a joining tool in all popular song since the nineteenth century, because it 'leads' naturally to the tonic, and so resolves any chord sequence back to the home key. It became a great cliché, and is much rarer now, because looped sequences cannot easily accommodate a dominant seventh chord every fourth bar. But as a joining device it still works well – as at the end of the middle section of *Roar* by Katy Perry – but it can sound a bit too dramatic in a groove-heavy track.

There are two chord sequences which do have names.

The first is very old – the 'cycle of fifths', which propped up baroque music, then appeared occasionally in songs such as *You Don't Have To Say You Love Me* by Dusty Springfield, and the magnificent *I Will Survive* by Gloria Gaynor. It is based on a descending series of root notes spaced in fifths – i.e. in C minor it would be F minor B flat E flat A flat, resolving back to the tonic via D minor 7th flat 5, G to C. It opens up beautiful melodic possibilities but has fallen into disuse. Until Adele revived it in *Million Years Ago*.

The second has a better pop history – the twelve-bar. There were many minor variations in the form, but here is a classic twelve-bar set out by the root note of its chords.

1 1 1 1

4 4 1 1

5 4 1 5

Examples include *Wooly Bully* by Sam the Sham and the Pharaohs and *The Wanderer* by Dion.

Though it involves only the 1 4 and 5 root notes, this form has an undeniable genius. It uses a different chord at the start of each 4-bar line, thus constantly refreshing the ear and reframing the melody; its harmonic rhythms intensifies, moving from a four-bar change in line 1, to a two-bar in line 2, then one-bar changes in the last line; it lacks symmetry, using not sixteen bars but twelve, which makes it edgier as a repeat cycle; and it ends on the dominant seventh, which gives the sequence a perfect handover to the start of the next verse.

The twelve-bar was heavily used in the 1950s. Elvis Presley, Little Richard, Bill Haley and many others had stacks of hits with it, and it enjoyed a long afterlife; *Kiss* by Prince and *Black Or White* by Michael Jackson are good later examples. Traces of it can still be found today – as in *Rehab* by Amy Winehouse or *bad guy* by Billie Eilish – but the classic form is now largely disused.

One other harmonic pattern is worthy of mention – the descending bass. This is basically a four-bar change from the tonic to the dominant seventh, during which the bass moves downwards in steps from 1 to 5. The effect is both tense and fluid, and allows scope for melody while retaining rhythmic power and heaviness. Very commonly used in the 1960s, it has largely disappeared, but can be heard in *Everybody* by Backstreet Boys, *Brain Stew* by Green Day and *Feeling Good* by Muse.

Other standard shapes include:

1 6 2 minor 5 – the classic swing jazz vamp, also to be found in *Mercy Mercy Me* by Marvin Gaye, and the chorus of *History* by One Direction

1 6 minor 4 5 – which supported a host of 1950s hits such as *All I Have to Do Is Dream* by The Everly Brothers or *Oh! Carol* by Neil Sedaka

1 5 6 minor 4 – a modern staple which appears in a vast range of songs from *You're Beautiful* by James Blunt, to *Don't Matter* by Akon and *Say You Won't Let Go* by James Arthur.

You don't need to use any of these templates, and you don't have to start your chord sequence on 1, as all these examples do. But it is a good idea to keep any sequence modally consistent, so you don't have to keep changing the key of your melody within it.

Essentially, the thing to notice here is not the specific chords in these four illustrations, but that their bass movements all follow one key/mode, which makes melody writing and cycling easier. This applies in either major or minor moods, as in the 1 minor 4 minor 6 5 minor of *Careless Whisper* by George Michael.

Make sure that your bass movements follow the master key/mode of your melody.

Chapter 7

Melody

A melody is a connected line of single notes – a tune. But not every linear arrangement of notes can be described as a melody, because a melody does something extra to us – it attracts and holds our attention. It has an internal logic that we are drawn to follow.

A well written melody will catch and retain our attention because it is full of disguised or subliminal repeat patterns – cells, motifs or catches – which provide internal emphasis and propel its development.

Melody, therefore, is better understood as a principle – as the organising sub-structure that holds a hummable tune together. The proportion and pacing of a good melody enables our brains to understand that these notes are somehow inherently related.

Melodies, therefore, are not merely top lines *over* music. A good melody can appear anywhere across the pitch range. There is as much melody in the bassline of *Walking on the Moon* by The Police as in the chorus of *Barbie Girl* by Aqua.

Well written songs often have a melodic arrangement as well as a good tune, and the two can actively help each other. Records by Abba and The Beatles are packed with melodic ideas buried in the arrangements. They act as secondary hooks, but really they are indispensable elements of the piece which work as counterparts and additions to the song's main melodic thrust.

A good vocal melody dictates the tempo of a song and directs the most prominent features of its arrangement. Melody also acts as the prime source of emotional connection to the audience, because it works in combination with words that channel our thoughts and feelings, which in a good performance will be rendered even more intense. No wonder melodies are so important.

The problem is in articulating exactly how all this works, and here again we come up against a fog of unknowing. There is no simple universally successful way to write a melody.

To be frank, great melodies are rare, and people who write them usually end up famous. But it is not necessary to be able to write truly great melodies to be a successful writer. A good pop melody doesn't have to aspire to greatness, it just needs to be neat and memorable – to have force. And everyone can write better melodies with practice and reflection.

Melodies are subject to fashion, but there are some fundamental principles which allow a good melody to work over decades, or even centuries. Listening to good melodies can teach us a great deal. They have nothing to hide – all their virtues are on display.

To this end, it is worth studying nursery rhymes, which act as a library of good melodic practice. They have almost ideal forms. The names of the writers may be lost, but what they were doing is what modern songwriters are still doing, but doing with a veneer of coolness applied to the lyrical content, and a distinct fashion statement in presentation. The virtues of simplicity and balance are the same.

Nursery rhymes are generally set out in combinations of four lines, just like a standard pop verse. Each line usually has a degree of symmetry to it, like *Rock-a-bye Baby*, or uses an exact repeat, like *Frère Jacques*, or the first two lines mirror each other, like *Twinkle Twinkle Little Star*. Or they use an AABA format, like *Au Clair de la Lune*, in which lines 1, 2 and 4 use the same tune with different words, while line 3 features a change of chord and melodic shape, but uses an almost identical rhythm to the other three lines. A bit like *Happy Birthday*, in fact. Note how often the exact rhythm of the first phrase of a melody is reproduced in the second: *Humpty Dumpty*, *The Dam Busters March*, *The Star-Spangled Banner*, *Norwegian Wood*. The pitches can be the same or different; that is your choice as a writer.

The universality of this form is perhaps best illustrated by the absence of its opposite. It is very hard to think of famous melodies that have radically different rhythms in their first two lines, whereas it is very common for rhythms to be identical while carrying different pitches.

Here we can find something more like an obvious truth than a secret: that melodies are actually closer to rhythmic than to harmonic patterns. This is another reason not to get too hung up about chords.

If you want to write a good melody, plan it, construct it and find chords that work with it as you go. Don't write a sequence of chords, then expect the melody to emerge either from its upper notes, or from simply reciting chord tones as they occur.

It's helpful to think in balanced phrases, taking care how they relate to each other. Look for patterns that have an obvious coherence, that carry a sense of internal binding. This should be like writing words that rhyme; if words don't rhyme immediately, they won't rhyme afterwards, no matter how long you wait.

The concept of rhyme in melody is as important as it is within lyric writing. Rhymes are sonic correspondences that mark out meter and structure. Writing melodies that rhyme should be your objective. If you can't hear any rhyme, keep going – you're not there yet.

When writing a melodic phrase, thinking in two- or three-note groups can help you to build up naturally balanced patterns. A phrase of two notes can create tension by repetition, or it can have movement – either up or down. A three-note phrase is more interesting because it can repeat, go one way, or both – up-down or down-up. A four-note phrase can be two twos, or a three and a one, or a one and a three. One note can't really be a phrase, but a pause after it can open up space which gives energy and shape to the phrases that follow. "I...I who have nothing". "You...shook me all night long."

A good melody sets itself up very quickly, by the use of distinct rhythms and intervals which lay out a template for subsequent lines. Dozens of famous melodies start like this.

Broadway songs are very clear in this aspect, and Leonard Bernstein had a gift. Several of the songs in *West Side Story* start by establishing these two key elements – interval and metric pattern. *Tonight*, *Maria*, *Somewhere* and *America* all do. Sting does this repeatedly, but melodies set up like this are rare in recent years.

Too much vertical movement in a melody can sound weak against a heavy beat, so one-note melodies are sometimes a better option than a series of sculpted intervals. Taylor Swift has deployed one-note melodies to advantage; clever people have counted over two hundred on her *1989* album. The chorus of *Tubthumping* by Chumbawumba uses no less than twenty-nine identical pitches in a row. *I Predict A Riot* by the Kaiser Chiefs and *Shout Out to My Ex* by Little Mix are less extravagant, but the idea goes back a long way, via The Beatles – the verse of *Strawberry Fields Forever*, the pre-chorus of *Lucy in the Sky with Diamonds*, the chorus of *All You Need Is Love*, the middle section of *Girl*, plus many others – to the verse of *Long Tall Sally* by Little Richard. As top lines these are all very incisive and insistent.

A special case has to be made for melody within soul music, where the written line is often just a starting point for ornamentation. This means that soul melody has become rather different from pop melody in certain crucial ways.

A good soul vocal relies on technical execution and, above all, intensity of feeling within the voice. These performance-based qualities are hard to write directly into a top line, and are best captured rather than truly written.

However, it is worth pointing out that the most successful writers in r&b write vocal lines which have clear shapes in their construction; for instance, Ashford and Simpson, LA and Babyface, or Jam and Lewis.

A brief soul heads-up. In the pentatonic scale, any bass note fits with any melody note. Easy. But because all notes work with each other in the pentatonic world, you must supply some other structure to make a strong melody. The best way is to be very definite about rhythm. Next best, avoid slurring and elision; use distinctive intervals. A pentatonic melody has no real purchase on chords, so it must have either defined pitch or rhythm of its own. If it has neither, it is essentially in free space, and is unlikely to cut through to a listener's memory.

Prince was an absolute genius at stamping rhythm on a soul melody, as in *Sign 'O' The Times*, *Hot Thing*, *Gett Off*, *Slave*, *Chocolate Box*, or *Black Sweat*. More subtly, he liked to give himself extra melodic freedom by refusing to define chords as either major or minor; the third step of the scale is often missing in his instrumental parts.

When writing any vocal melody, work with small groups of notes in distinct, matching feet, like short-long or long-short-short. Recently, a short-short on the first two semiquavers of the bar has become fashionable. Confined to funk bass riffs in the 1970s, it has now appeared in numerous r&b vocal lines, as at the end of the chorus of *thank u, next*, where Ariana frankly expresses her gratitude to her exes.

Make sure that your melody has defined shape and internal correspondences. Don't just play it on a keyboard; sing it without accompaniment to satisfy yourself that it sounds strong on its own, not just when carried by your beat, or floating over your chords.

Chapter 8

Lyrics

Above and beyond music, words give a song three specific ways to connect with a listener.

First, words create mental links in a way that music simply cannot. Music is essentially abstract, and to carry any precise meaning it needs to derive it from words. Second, words allow an artist an extra layer of distinctive expression beyond musical and visual style, allowing exhibitions of skill and insight that are in themselves a form of entertainment, and can appeal directly to a target audience. Lastly, if a lyric describes familiar feelings in new language, it makes a song unmistakeably current.

Words thus give songs meaning, character and a location in time and place – in sum, an identity.

But a good lyric does not have to say anything deep; its main function is to appear as integrated with the music as possible. Oscar-winning lyricist Don Black once said that a good lyric should "hug the contours of a melody". Profundity is a bonus.

A lyric corresponds in many ways to an instrumental part. It is a subsidiary element which should be integrated within the arrangement – and it should be self-consistent. It shouldn't jump out, but it should carry some weight in the final product.

A bad lyric won't douse a musical fire, and a really clever lyric won't save boring music. Industry people will point out that there are plenty of hit records with lousy lyrics, but no hit records with lousy music. A successful popular song is always a partnership, tilted slightly towards the music.

When they rise above the banal, lyrics have a lot in common with poetry (prosody, imagery and compressed forms), and all the classic poetic devices are available to writers, including simile, metaphor, irony, analogy, antithesis, paradox, characterization and personification. However, there is no need to get overly concerned about fancy language.

The most important way in which words collaborate with music is in stressing 'parallel' or matching sounds. These give internal structure to a melody, and can mark out the boundaries of a couplet, verse or chorus.

Lyrical devices can usefully be broken down into three, in terms of their function.

1. Devices which make internal links by the use of repetition. Rhyme is the stressed repeat of a syllable ending: night/right. Assonance is the repeat of any vowel sound: blue moon. Alliteration is the repeat of an initial consonant: baby blue.

These are devices that collate *sounds* to create structure.

Vowels are the key; they are naturally singable. Consonants have no pitched value, but can carry musical stress and enhance rhythm.

Emphasis on the syllable before the end of a line is called 'feminine' rhyme, whereas hitting the end is called 'masculine'. Switching these around a little can help add more interesting rhythms. Sean Paul's *Get Busy* features rhymes on beat 3 of the bar, and has been extensively imitated.

Rappers became very aware of how the ending of a rhymed line can be a giant anti-climax ('old school'), and began patterning their lines to carry much more internal stress, with heavy use of assonance. Check out *Rap God* by Eminem.

Never use words just because they rhyme. Rhyme should always be at the service of meaning. And don't twist word order to force a rhyme; this calls attention to itself in a bad way.

Rhyme also has a powerfully predictive quality – it inevitably casts its influence forwards. Once listeners get used to the pattern, they are waiting for the rhyme. If you rhyme the first two lines of a verse the expectation will be that the next two lines will rhyme too (AABB), so you have added predictability while losing flexibility. In verses, more open forms, such as ABCB, may be better.

It is generally a good idea to use different rhyme schemes in a verse and chorus. AABB works well in a chorus precisely because it is emphatic.

Assonance is now more prevalent than ever, especially with the rise of rap styles, which are greedy for sonic correspondences that help create patterns of stress. Rhymes are also much looser in current pop songs. *Love Yourself* by Justin Bieber only has one perfect rhyme in the whole song (small/all).

American-English pronunciation has tended to mix up rhyme and assonance. Going back over classic songs we can find pairings such as friend/again, tent/since, time/line, public/subject, Duke/lose, kitchen/ambition.

Alex Turner of Arctic Monkeys is probably the best current British exponent of assonance. For example, *Do I Wanna Know?* is a veritable symphony in 'ee'.

Alliteration is a marginal benefit. It can add smoothness to a line, and it binds adjectives to nouns – 'sweet summer sweat'. It also helps titles – Suffragette City, Karma Chameleon – but in musical terms, alliteration is a bit of a luxury.

Starting several lines with the same word or phrase (epibole or anaphrasis), is *structural* rhyme. It is a simple way of adding extra emphasis – a form of double repeat – of sound and of placement. Examples: *Cannonball*, by Damien Rice, *Because* by The Beatles, *Money* by Pink Floyd, *She* by Charles Aznavour, and *Panic* by The Smiths.

2. Devices which make internal links by using comparisons and contrasts.

A simile is a direct comparison that is real and observable. A metaphor is a comparison that is not real, but rings true in a poetic sense. Antithesis is a direct contrast between two things – ideas, people or conditions.

These are devices that link *ideas*, not sounds.

Comparisons need to have an element of truth in them, unless they are intentionally absurd or humorous. Contrasts have less allegiance to truth. They deliver shock value, and are an open road to humour and paradox, which can add vitality and depth to a lyric.

Similes use a direct joining word, 'as' or 'like'.

> I came in like a wrecking ball
>
> ***Wrecking Ball***, Miley Cyrus
> (Maureen Anne McDonald, Sacha Skarbek, Lukasz Gottwald, Henry Russell Walter, Kim Kiyani, Stephan Moccio © Sony/ATV Music Publishing LLC, Universal Music Publishing Group, Downtown Music Publishing)

Metaphors rely on transformation, by describing one thing as if it were another. They say something about the world that is not literally true, which cannot be seen but can be pointed out and is revealing in some way. They work as a form of secret, shared knowledge.

> You're my kryptonite

> You keep making me weak
>
> ***One Thing***, One Direction
> (Savan Harish Kotecha, Rami Yacoub, Carl Anthony Falk © Kobalt Music Publishing Ltd., Sony/ATV Music Publishing LLC, BMG Rights Management, Ole Media Management Lp)

Metaphors are best when they communicate at a single shot. If you have a good one, put it in the chorus, as a summation, so that you can explain and exploit it in the rest of the lyric.

For a clear distinction between a simile and a metaphor: You eat like a pig – simile: You are a pig – metaphor. Two things become one in the metaphor.

Antithesis directly opposes two things and can be expressed either in a 'this-that' form, or can be couched in metaphorical terms.

> Dry house, wet clothes
>
> ***The A Team***, Ed Sheeran
> (© Sony/ATV Music Publishing LLC)
>
> You go back to her and I go back to black
>
> ***Back To Black***, Amy Winehouse
> (Amy Winehouse, Mark Ronson © Sony/ATV Music Publishing LLC, BMG Rights Management)

Antithesis is very useful because of its brevity and directness. It has a summarising effect, and is probably the quickest way to sound wise about the world, or yourself and your situation.

And it is not hard to find; it is lurking everywhere, in every binary opposition, of which there are plenty in human perceptions: big small, alive dead, hot cold, me you, up down, here there, first last, rich poor, happy sad, right wrong, yes no, come go etc.

Personal relationships suggest a great many other oppositions. Some can be strongly antithetical, others merely comparative.

> However I look, it's clear to see
> That I love you more than you love me
>> ***Getting Away With It***, Electronic
>> (Jodi Marr, Jodi M. Horovitz, Simon Bass © Warner Chappell Music, Inc, Universal Music Publishing Group)

> Don't forget me, I beg, I remember you said
> Sometimes it lasts in love, but sometimes it hurts instead
>> ***Someone Like You***, Adele
>> (Adele Laurie Blue Adkins, Daniel Dodd Wilson © Sony/ATV Music Publishing LLC, Universal Music Publishing Group, BMG Rights Management)

A very productive area is the interplay of tenses. The potential contrasts between the three worlds of past, present and future have kept writers busy for years with bittersweet juxtapositions: old new, then now, bad better.

> There's no tenderness like before in your fingertips
>> ***You've Lost That Lovin' Feelin'***, The Righteous Brothers
>> (Phil Spector, Barry Mann, Cynthia Weil © Sony/ATV Music Publishing LLC)

Antithesis is more self-explanatory than metaphor, and frequently more entertaining. It is also more intrinsically rhythmic, because it has two distinct, sequential elements that can fit well across or within lines.

3. One-off devices, such as characterization and personification, which supply details to illuminate the meaning of the song, set out its emotional landscape and intensify the interaction of its main players. These propel the narrative and add physical context.

There is a hierarchy of effectiveness within these various devices.

Similarities are weaker than contrasts, a fact we can all recognise from our experience of music. Contrasts constantly refresh themselves.

Straight similes can be very banal: white as snow. Try to use some imagination, irony or mischief.

> You're about as easy as a nuclear war
>
> ***Is There Something I Should Know?,*** Duran Duran
>
> (Andy Taylor, Gordon Brown, John Taylor, Nick Rhodes, Robert Harold Tanico, Roger Taylor, Simon Le Bon © Sony/ATV Music Publishing LLC)

'Than' is a more powerful conjunction than 'as' or 'like'. It allows more flexible fun than a straight comparison. Statements in the form of "I am as high as a kite" are literal and therefore limited. "I'm higher than a kite" leaves more for the listener to do with the image.

In other words, a simile is less interesting than an open-ended comparison – hotter than July, *slicker than* an oil spill, smoother than a fresh jar of Skippy.

One-off devices give style and depth, but they are the least important element in any lyric. They are specific to a particular song and don't have much of a life when taken out of context.

Writers should try to mix up the available devices; they should not be thought of as separate, like keys, but more like notes in a harmonious chord.

> You always smiled but in your eyes your sorrow showed, yes it showed
>> ***Without You***, Harry Nilsson
>> (Tom Evans, Pete Ham © BMG Rights Management, Songtrust Ave, Kobalt Music Publishing Ltd.)

Assonance, alliteration, antithesis, characterization, personification, and repetition.

> All together, all alone…
> Until that night you passed by
> Hand in hand with another guy
> Dressed to kill, and guess who's dying
>> ***Dance Away***, Roxy Music
>> (Bryan Ferry © Universal Music Publishing Group)

Epibole, compression, repetition, alliteration, irony. The last line converts the rhyme from a masculine to a feminine form, leaving a feeling of incompleteness, giving a softer, more elongated effect to the word 'dying'.

> You're in my blood like holy wine
>> ***A Case Of You***, Joni Mitchell
>> (© Crazy Crow Music / Siquomb Music Publishing)

Part of the song's extended metaphor about alcohol, but also an allusion to Holy Communion, salvation and obsession.

If you're under him
You're not getting over him

> *New Rules*, Dua Lipa
> (Caroline Ailin, Emily Warren, Ian Kirkpatrick © Warner Chappell Music, Inc, Peermusic Publishing, BMG Rights Management, Warner Chappell Music Inc.)

Antithesis, paradox, summative.

Good actors try to 'own the intelligence' of their characters, i.e. to have their thoughts in real time. In lyric writing you are also trying to own the intelligence of your audience. Give them the right material, in the right order, at the right speed. This is the deeper level of the classic 'who what when where' approach.

The best story songs usually introduce or locate at least two characters and a place and time in their first line or couplet. Examples: *Ode To Billie Joe* by Bobbie Gentry, *Lola* by The Kinks, *Don't You Want Me* by The Human League. This type of song is currently out of fashion, except in country music, but, as ever with fashion, this presents opportunities for writers.

If you have a stonking good lyrical idea, put it in the second verse. If you put it in the first, and you have no equivalent follow-up, the second verse might sound a bit flat. First verses take care of themselves.

Using proverbs – folk wisdom – has the virtue of familiarity, though it can sound banal. Motown writers often did this, putting cliché at the service of easy communication: *You Can't Hurry Love, Too Many Fish In The Sea, Needle In A Haystack, Stop, Look, Listen*.

But proverbs can work well if you twist them a little:

> They say you gotta stay hungry

Hey baby, I'm just about starving tonight

> ***Dancing In The Dark***, Bruce Springsteen
> (© Universal Music Publishing Group)

Chapter 9

Creative Practicalities

Now we can return to the four decisions that shape the creative process: what shall I do, how do I start, what do I do next, and when is it finished?

These are all difficult and persistent questions, but self-awareness as a writer will help you find answers to all of them in context.

"What shall I do?" is clearly a more fundamental question than all the others. Sometimes, while in the middle of a body of work – either as an individual or as part of a group – the answer will be obvious. You are asked to write a song with or for a particular artist, you need another track for your album, you are pitching for an end-roller song for a film. But at other times there can be real difficulties in conceiving new work before you have started it.

The big ideas are the hardest to come by, yet they often take a very small amount of time when they arrive. It is difficult to formalise this process.

When answering the other three questions, progress can always be made by clear thinking and hard work. This is the realm of what can be called 'constructive prejudice' – a standard of personal judgement that you build up through experience, reflection and listening to music with active curiosity.

You need to develop constructive prejudice because creativity relies on making chains of decisions. Some are rational and practical; this note, that word. Others are framed by random events. You might play a wrong note, or paste a part in an unexpected place, or mishear what someone else says. Is this a lucky chance that helps you, or an annoyance to be ignored? You can only decide by developing a clear sense of what you do and don't like.

It is perfectly natural that certain things seem pleasing to you while others do not. Even if you cannot rationalise your musical tastes, which are just cognitive biases, you can accept and internalise them. If you do this thoroughly, you can speed through small decision forks while you are writing, leaving you free to concentrate on the big decisions that truly affect the overall quality of a piece of work.

Prejudice in social interactions is limiting and damaging, but in an artistic context, prejudice is the very lifeblood of *style*. Prejudice within the creative arts simply means preferring one outcome to another. If every outcome is equal to you, how can you make decisions? And, more importantly, how can you make chains of consistent decisions?

Songwriters cannot treat all ideas as equal. Either/or choices must be made. So, work out what you like, by listening or active imitation, or by joining forces with others and discussing where your tastes overlap. Good bands do this, and their collective ability to cover each other's weaknesses and promote each other's strengths makes a band distinctive.

Develop your own personal playbook. It need not be entirely rational, but it should reflect you – the way you do things as opposed to anyone else. This is an even more pressing priority in an era when everyone has the same equipment.

Now: "How do I start?" There are ten classic starting points for a song: a title, a beat, a lyric, a melody, a hook, a mood/vibe, a chord movement, an instrumental part, an artist you have in mind, a direct commission.

Any of these can get you going, but the best is probably a strong melody, and the most compelling is a direct commission. The worst, from a song writing point of view, is a beat, because a beat can do both too much and too little. It can be too satisfying too quickly, leaving you feeling that the work is already done. Remember, any beat wears thin over three minutes.

"What do I do next?" This is vitally important in influencing a whole chain of events. There are no rules; context is everything. But in general, whatever it is you do, you should only add something that excites or truly satisfies you. If you do this consistently, you are raising the bar within the material. Doing the opposite – settling for second best – risks letting inferior ideas pass muster as good.

"When is it finished?" This isn't a snap decision. It's finished when you are satisfied you can't make it any better. If you are recording a master, this is a production decision. At the writing stage, you should be satisfied that all the sections work well individually and in sequence.

To judge that, you must learn to recognise when you've done something good. The only way out of guesswork is to develop your own taste and be strict about it. You can then apply a consistent reference to your output, which will give you licence to do something simple and recognise that it has value, or is appropriate for the purpose you intend. In the room, it will always be your personal judgement that comes first, so this really matters. If you need someone else to tell you what is right, you will be in a very slow feedback system, like trying to solve Rubik's Cube in a dark cupboard and occasionally stepping outside to ask someone how you're doing.

Hero worship is no great help. It tends to switch off both your emotional and analytical senses. Remember, you are on your own, in your own time and space.

It is easy to feel that your idols were somehow superior. But don't imagine that they didn't struggle with the same constraints that seem to be thwarting you. Yes, they were possessed of a superior something, but it was not an abstract talent. Mostly they were clearer in their minds about what they were doing, at least in patches, and they did not let mundane concerns intrude, though they would certainly have been there. They too had money worries, diary problems, ill health, malfunctioning equipment, difficult emotional lives, and degrees of public indifference or even hostility. Jimi Hendrix wrote *The Wind Cries Mary* after a row with his girlfriend about mashed potato.

When it comes to heroes, don't do what they did; think like they thought.

The power of collective energy should not be underestimated, and working in a team is generally quicker and more fun than writing alone. Collaboration is now very common at the top end of the writing profession, because of the speed and sustained quality it offers. But all groups and individuals hit moments when the ideas dry up, when hard decisions have to be made, when it is no longer obvious what should be done.

Some decisions are taken very quickly, in moments of clarity and elation. But deciding between options, or trying to figure out how an idea should develop can be very time consuming, as it is often difficult to know immediately when you are getting it right. Usually you need to travel a little way along any path to convince yourself that it's the best way forward.

When in doubt, always sing a song out loud with energy. This can be very revealing about problems of structural balance, excess complexity, comprehensibility – and breathing.

Instinct here is probably more useful than technique, though technique is always helpful in solving problems, because it gives you options. But ultimately you must base your decisions on criteria like directness and effective communication, not cleverness or advanced musical or lyrical facility.

If you are working in a team, you need a good balance between yes people and no people. Too much positivity can mean lower standards, and the bigger picture risks getting scrambled. But too much negativity leads to dead ends, glum faces, and hurt feelings. "Yes, but…" is always better than a plain "No". Bouncing ideas around so that no one owns them is a good idea. Then no one sulks, everyone stays excited and remains eager to contribute.

Creativity is a multi-speed activity, because there are both big and little steps within it, and the little steps cannot be overlooked. The devil really is in the detail. Looking back over a writing session, not all the time was equally valuable, but you probably had to go through all of it to get to the point of creation – that is the nature of the journey.

It is important to unpack and distinguish two concepts – originality and distinctiveness. In the pop world it is only necessary to have the second. And not even that is actually necessary for success of some kind. But for sustained success, and for recognition as a significant contributor to the tradition, distinctiveness is by far the more important.

Successful songwriters use familiar rhythms and chords, and it is hardly possible to have new emotions that no human being has felt before. There are certainly new experiences opening up to humanity – seeing the Earth from outer space is one; contact with people in new environments such as the internet is another. But do these generate truly new emotions, or simply variations on old ones?

There is scarcely one original idea in the catalogues of either Oasis or The Electric Light Orchestra, but they are entirely recognisable as artists. The most valuable asset is the ability to say something familiar in a way that is truly your own. In this sense, Lemmy of Motörhead is as important and instructive a role model as pioneers like Björk or Kanye West. We are not reinventing the wheel, but we can design attractive new tyres for it.

Now for three myths.

First, not everyone has the same amount of talent. This is not the message usually sent out by on-line tutorials or self-help books, but it is nearer the truth than telling everyone that they can tap into their previously unsuspected genius or unleash their inner rock star. But it is possible to make the most of what talent you possess, especially in combinations.

Next, musical knowledge does not kill creativity. It can and should help in a way that ignorance never can. Theoretical knowledge gives you more approaches, and more shades to use in your song picture. Similarly, mastery of technology – effects, pedals, automated mixing, sound design, or even open tunings – allows you to go where no one else has been. Trevor Horn is the exemplar. He was not just a good writer but also a brilliantly innovative producer who quite deliberately took technology further than any of his contemporaries.

Finally, the myth of the magic formula.

Successful writers often have patterns within their output – proof that they have their habits and preferences – and prejudices. For instance, none of Chic's big hits had pre-choruses. But neither David Bowie nor Prince had patterns at all; they were restless souls in search of constant reinvention.

At present, the most commonly touted myth is about Max Martin, the astoundingly successful writer-producer behind hits by Britney Spears, Katy Perry, Taylor Swift, The Weeknd and many others. He once mentioned that he uses 'melodic math' in his writing, but neglected to explain what he meant. Analysis of his hits reveals that he often writes in major keys, seldom uses more than five chords in a song, and usually gets to his first chorus at around 42 seconds. But this is all fluff. It is not these things that make his records successful.

What does? It is talent, taste and experience, all of which he has in abundance. He admits that he always prioritises vocal content, and we know from listening that he maintains a clear focus of attention within a song and makes regular and effective use of contrasts. More subtly, his songs feature heavy vocal repetitions, but with additions and positional shifts which add interest to a song's later stages, and usually emphasise its title. We many never know what melodic math is, and it really doesn't matter. Max Martin's approach is all about message discipline.

You can easily find patterns in any writer's output for yourself. Count bars, note the order of sections and pick out repeat structures in words and music. Listen and learn; great writers are all great teachers. The main lesson is – don't be boring.

Chapter 10

Approaching the Business

The music business is always in need of songs, which gives you your chance. But the business has long-standing systems in place to provide it with suitable material. Therefore, if you want to sell your songs, they must be competitive.

So, how should new writers approach the business? The answer depends on a number of personal factors; for instance, what genre you fit into, and where you live. But the biggest and most relevant question is whether you see yourself as a recording artist who intends to write your own material, or as a writer who is willing to write for/with artists within their careers.

As a potential artist you should approach a record company, whereas writers should approach a publisher. Getting a publishing deal as an artist is much easier if you already have a recording contract.

If you want to be a self-contained artist, you must convince the industry that you have a viable future, and your first objective must be to assemble proof positive of your popularity. Live playing is no longer the only way to build an audience, though it speaks for itself if you can. Nowadays internet stats allow record companies to quantify an artist's following. So, attend to your social media presence.

Your second, and rather more important objective, is to generate unarguably strong material. Far too many people embark upon attracting industry attention when they are not ready. Have at least three well-produced, consistent songs to show. If you have not sorted out your genre, your style, your look, your personnel, then hold back. It is no good touting around recordings for which you have to make excuses – I had a cold, we've got a new drummer since then, we ran out of money to finish the mix etc. Show yourself at your best.

It is a myth that the music industry signs artists on potential. It doesn't, it signs artists on excitement. So make sure that what you present is compelling.

Nor does the industry sign long shots; originality is not a great virtue in its eyes. It likes to back short odds with heavy money, and then, if possible, to rig the race as well – a process called promotion, which is very expensive.

The business will only spend its money to back its own judgement, so if you want to maintain a completely independent stance you will have to back your own judgement with your own money. This is not impossible, and unsigned artists have ended up with chart success, even number one records. But it is unusual. Self-financed artists have to rely on quality and personality to compete. and trying to go it alone is not really a viable strategy for a whole career.

Before you approach the industry, you must do everything you possibly can to polish and refine your music. Internal coherence within the project, a clearly defined sound and direction, and excellent visual presentation are essential to excite industry people who, naturally, have entirely rational doubts and fears when strangers come into their offices. Are these the people who made this recording? Is it their copyright to dispose of? Can they do it again?

Basic personal honesty has to be in place about the copyright issue, but the question of repeatability can only be answered by producing more material. If you present one song, the first thing you will be asked to do is to bring more, as quickly as possible. And any industry person worth their salt will absolutely insist on seeing the act live. A successful gig dispels a lot of doubts; yes, the act has a following; yes, it really is the singer who sang on the recording; yes, he/she looks great and exudes confidence from the stage, and yes, people do love that song.

It is important to understand that talent scouts do not use their imagination. The reason is simple. If you start imagining things that aren't there, that the songs could be improved if... that the singer could be better with a few lessons... that the band's sound could be refined in the studio... then suddenly you are signing a fantasy construct that you have invented yourself. Don't expect industry people to use their imaginations; they can't afford to. If they did, they would sign everything. They have to be convinced.

So be absolutely clear about yourself. Don't confuse biz people with your 'versatility', or leave decisions to them that you should be making for yourself. You want to be your own creation, not theirs. And if you put the onus on them, they won't decide; they'll just pass.

Things are rather different if you present yourself as a writer.

You are basically asking a publisher to take a bet on whether your material could fit into a successful artist's career. This is less a question of the song's absolute artistic worth, and more a matter of judging it by comparisons – it sounds very current, it sounds a bit like another hit. This kind of positive comparison can help persuade industry people that your song, too, has commercial appeal.

It is asking a lot of a publisher to sign up a catalogue of eccentric songs if you do not intend to sing them yourself; the only conceivable use for those songs will be your own recording career. Therefore, if you intend to write for the open market, you must present plainly marketable songs. You can be very non-specific about this, and consciously write material that could be covered by any pop act.

Or you can write songs that you think would be suitable for a particular high-profile artist, though this comes with a few problems of its own.

The first is that successful artists already have sources of good material available to them, so your song has to be outstanding. Remember, it is always in the financial interests of artists (and producers) to record their own mediocre material rather than your mediocre material.

The next problem is that whatever you write for your named artist, you will have based it on that artist's previous output. This automatically puts you in a different mind-set from them. They are focused on their next album, while you will be writing what could sound to them like legacy material. This is probably not what they want. And if the artist is looking to evolve, it is unlikely that you will accurately predict their change of direction. If you sent a *Single Ladies* sound-alike to Beyoncé while she was recording the *Lemonade* album, it would have got a chilly reception. No self-respecting artist is going to base their future direction on material from someone they've never heard of.

Big name artists, especially if they have control over their own careers (and most these days do) may prove resistant to taking on 'outside' material, especially from newbies. The artists who really need good material are the ones who have not yet figured out how to provide it for themselves, and these are likely to be lower profile record company-sponsored pop acts, either solo artists or boy/girl bands.

This means that your material probably won't end up with Beyoncé, and is more likely to find its way to a new artist whose record company thinks she sounds a bit like a young Beyoncé. You may well get your cover, but it might not be at the level you hoped for.

The lesson here is that if you want to write eclectic or progressive material you are better off trying to front it yourself as an artist. Or if you feel you are not a viable artist yourself, you can find a singer/front person with whom to collaborate, and divide up the performing, writing and producing duties between you.

If you want to avoid going down either of these routes, both of which are convoluted and risky, you are better advised to stick to mainstream, centre-ground pop, and write songs that anyone with an ear can take on.

Lastly, a warning. The fringes of the music business play host to a legion of hustlers and scammers ready to take your money rather than develop your talent.

Avoid anyone who tells you there is a secret formula for hit songs, and that they know it. A moment's reflection will tell you this is nonsense. Styles change all the time, so what was good for 2018 will not necessarily work in 2022. And if these people know this precious, infallible formula, why are they selling it to you for a few dollars when they could be making hits and earning millions?

Avoid anyone who claims that they can promote your material on-line, with, for example, guaranteed followers, streams, hits, support slots, PAs, and radio plays.

Just. Not. True.

Do it yourself. It may be slower, but it has a better chance of working out right for you. You are more likely to be noticed by the high priests at Spotify by consistently releasing good quality material yourself.

If you think you need a manager, choose one who has both experience and time to devote to you. Also, make sure your contract has an early break clause and some performance criteria written into it.

Proper music biz people will not ask for your money; they expect to take a cut from what you bring in over the long term. Anyone who seems to be trying to do anything else should he regarded with deep suspicion.

Song writing remains in many ways a mysterious process, but reflection and persistence are both essential elements of success. This book has aimed to help with reflection, but persistence is down to you.

One last, and crucially important secret, is that you should always try to satisfy yourself first. Buddy Holly once said: "I don't know how to succeed, but I know how to fail: try to please everybody, that'll make you fail."

Two final rules to follow.

One: use repetition of form and variation of content in as many ways as you can, within melodic, lyrical and arrangement patterns. This gives continuity and focus.

Two: use musical contrasts, of texture, tonality and pace, and vocal contrasts, of range, quality and intensity. This gives variety and interest.

If you do, your songs will run more smoothly and be more memorable, and fewer ideas will hold the listener's attention for longer.

Good luck.

Twelve Take Aways

Use repetition of form and variation in content

Use types of repetition that are not exact

Vary pitch rather than rhythm

Your best source of originality is your own personality

Use what already exists and make it your own, in your time and place

Great songs are the ones that anybody can sing

Say things in your songs that people might want to have said for them

Use the rule of three in top-lines

Don't settle for second best. Drive up the bar, not to the bar

Average listeners don't hear or care about chords

Impose strict form on any pentatonic melody

Please yourself first

© Roddy Matthews 2020

Bite-Sized Lifestyle Books

Bite-Sized Lifestyle Books are designed to provide insights and ideas about our lives and the pressures on all of us and what we can do to change our environment and ourselves.

They are deliberately short, easy to read, books helping readers to gain a different perspective. They are firmly based on personal experience and where possible successful actions.

Bite-Sized Books don't cover every eventuality, but they are written from the heart by successful people who are happy to share their experience with you and give you the benefit of their success.

We have avoided jargon – or explained it where we have used it as a shorthand – and made few assumptions about the reader, except that they are literate and numerate, and that they can adapt and use what we suggest to suit their own, individual purposes.

Bite-Sized Books Catalogue

We publish Business Books, Life-Style Books, Public Affairs Books, including our Brexit Books, Fiction – both short form and long form – and Children's Fiction.

To see our full range of books, please go to
https://bite-sizedbooks.com/

Made in the USA
Monee, IL
11 December 2023